The Red Coat

Written by Roderick Hunt
Illustrated by Nick Schon,
based on the original characters
created by Roderick Hunt and Alex Brychta

OXFORD
UNIVERSITY PRESS

Read these words

coat soap

soak foam

king pongs

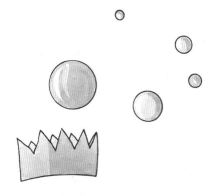

Chip was a king.

"I am a king," Chip said to Mum.

"I need a king's coat," he said.

Mum took Chip to a shop.

Chip put on a red coat.

The coat had an odd smell.

"Yuk. It smells odd," said Chip.

Chip put the coat in the tub.

"It can soak in the tub," he said.

Dad had a load of washing.

Chip put the coat in.

Dad's washing was red.

"Look at my washing," said Dad.

It's all red.

Chip was upset.

"But look at the coat," said Mum.

"He is the red king," said Mum.

Talk about the story

Spot the difference

Find the five differences in the two pictures of Chip.